Bursting with life and replete with colors, scents, flavors, and textures, the poems in Shirley J. Brewer's *Goddess of Swizzle* personify joie de vivre. They explore every corner of human experience, from vivid childhood memories to sobering adult losses, but joy is never far off. Here is a poet whose mirth at watching her mother squeeze into a girdle is as irrepressible as her sorrow, sipping a Manhattan at her father's grave. This collection is so refreshing, such an antidote to the world's miseries. "Forget decorum," Brewer advises—and she does. But beneath these poems' often playful surfaces beats the heart of a poet who knows what it means to be alive.

— Sue Ellen Thompson, author of *Sea Nettles: New & Selected Poems* and winner of the Maryland Author Award

By kindergarten Shirley J Brewer was already considered "sassy," but I think the nuns would have described her better as a girl with gusto. Gusto is the word William Hazlitt cites as the "power or passion defining any object." Brewer lives in a world of dazzling wonder and excitement. She eats the world alive. She finds "a festival of delight" in such strange and homely things as getting Juicy Fruit from the "secret place" in her Grandpa Joe's wooden leg. She quotes Martin Buber, "Play is the exultation of the possible," and her own world "glows in the resplendent light that makes all of us beautiful." Nowhere is that more evident than in her ekphrastic poems celebrating the sumptuousness of Matisse, and the dark convoluted spirals of Van Gogh's *The Starry Night*.

— David Bergman, author of *Plain Sight*, 2025 winner of the Towson Prize for Literature

With playful wisdom and kaleidoscopic language, Shirley J. Brewer invites the reader into a vibrant world where fire hydrants gush Kool Aid, mannequins yearn to walk, and the beloved dead return through the magic of memory. These delightful poems will make you feel better about being human.

— Jane Delury, author of *Hedge* and *The Balcony*

GODDESS OF SWIZZLE

Shirley J. Brewer

First Edition

Library of Congress Control Number: 2025948871

Paperback ISBN: 978-1-62720-624-2
Ebook ISBN: 978-1-62720-625-9

Printed in the United States of America

Design by Cecelia Durborow
Cover painting by Hal Boyd, used by permission
Author photo by Bonnie Schupp
Editorial Development by Olivia DiTroia
Promotional Development by Emily Gott

Published by Apprentice House Press

Apprentice House Press
Loyola University Maryland
4501 N. Charles Street
Baltimore, MD 21210
410.617.5265
www.ApprenticeHouse.com
info@ApprenticeHouse.com

Contents

For Snow Kim Collins
In loving memory of
Ted Adams and Judy K. Taylor

No easy thing to bear, the weight of sweetness.

—Li-Young Lee, The Weight of Sweetness

...and because you do not eat
that which rips your heart with joy.

—Thomas Lux, Refrigerator, 1957

The bar noise makes a kind of silence.

—Terrance Hayes, Cocktails with Orpheus

My Glass Slipper

Cinderella's legend beckoned
in that green land where I came to study poetry.

I found her shoe—kissed by a pink flower,
a golden heel—atop a pedestal

at a shop in Kinsale, a town on Ireland's
south coast. Pale blue storefronts

vied with lemon, lilac, lime. The air
tasted like candy and the sea.

A glass slipper so easily broken.
I held back. With a wave of his wand,

the shopkeeper wrapped my treasure
in safe cotton. Twenty-one years later,

I gaze at this fragile souvenir,
marvel at my perfect choice:

I am still a girl in love with words.
I dip my toes in the language of bards.

How long will a glass slipper carry me?
How far will I dare to walk?

A feast for here and now

Poem Beginning with a Line from Richard Hugo

**You might come here Sunday on a whim,*
after a whiskey sour brunch in Hampden
where everyone calls you *Hon.*
Witness the bold explosion. Isn't it rich
the way a woman revives her life?
Feast on feathery red lamps, a flamingo-
pink coffee table, lime pillows.
Light splashes in through tall windows.
Lavender high heels sequin the mantel.
Listen to the vibrant sounds
of sirens and the city.
You might wonder how someone
could move forward and away
from all the canyons of the past,
without a map, without a plan.

* "Degrees of Gray in Philipsburg"

A Taste of Lime

Forget laundry. In Costa Rica silken art
billows and bleeds on the clothes lines.

Primary hues riot in open air:
parakeet blues, a taste of lime,

an indiscretion of red—
I lose myself in a gauzy maze.

Butterflies, toucans, erotic petals
sizzle in heat. I soon succumb

to neon, become part of the prism.
Wrap me in a sea-scented scarf.

Drench my senses. No ordinary tourist,
bold fabrics replenish me.

Ban beige! I cry out,
my voice a tropical coloratura.

Self-Portrait in 22 Lines

Because I learn the Cartwheel Galaxy is 500 million
light-years from Earth,
I tether my story to numbers:

Age 2. In the front-page newspaper photo,
I'm holding a globe-shaped clock, a reminder to turn back the hour.
The caption claims: *She has time on her hands.*

Age 5. Grandma Alice gifts me a kaleidoscope.
This magic wand alive in my hands—slender
telescope revealing a universe of colored glass.

Age 7. I write fairy tales on lined school paper,
unfurling my imagination. My hand makes
punctuation marks like pinpricks, a map of tiny stars.

Ages 8-14. My trick-or-treat era. Hands toss Turkish Taffy,
Fireballs, Butterfingers and other candy bars into my bag.
I gravitate to Milky Ways.

Here is everything you need to know—how I catapult
from colors to words and back again, how schedules constrict.
Always, I want to cartwheel through Earth-years,
adrift in my own galaxy, my sweet time zone.
How bold I am to choose among 500 million
possibilities for poems. Such an astronomical array.
You might say: *She tries to capture a little sugar, a little light.*

Family Spirits

Dad drank Genesee Cream Ale
in moderation. He swigged one or two
cold brews on summer afternoons.
Winters, he mixed a mean Manhattan:
a tumble of maraschinos,
two smidgens of Vermouth.

Mom imbibed once in a while,
gladdened by Dad's Manhattans.
Dark days in upstate New York, ice
coated our wide driveway.
Inside, cubes clinked in pink crystal,
our living room alive with lamps.

How they raised a Kahlua daughter
remains a mystery. Black and White
Russians embellished my college years,
the coffee scent a zest, an exclamation.
Beer made me sick. Manhattan
meant a city, skyscraper gray.

Vacation photos render us compatible,
our cocktails a contrast: caramel Jim Beam,
Kahlua coal. Dad's witty toasts,
the way we brought nectar to our lips—
glasses meeting in mid-air. Holidays,
I continue our tradition, make Mom

a Manhattan, fix a companion drink for Dad.
Raising both tumblers high, I imagine my parents
sipping sweetness in a starry lounge
where the bartender never says *last call.*

Coming of Age in Wegmans

Every day you get our best.

Conceived in my hometown of Rochester, New York,
the magical market anchored my neighborhood.
First memory: riding in a grocery cart. I didn't mind
sharing space with a pineapple, limes, two gallons of milk.

Toddler years, I toyed with soup cans. By third grade,
I was well-adjusted to the meat counter—grisly steaks,
sausage necklaces, those hefty butchers dressed for Halloween
in red-stained aprons, squeaky shoes, bloodshot eyes. Later on

I earned straight A's for my food-list expertise,
marking off bargains my mother tossed into our wiry
Wegmans race car. Mom, an intense shopper, once cracked a rib
leaning over for a hidden quart of Butterscotch Ripple.

Upper grades caught me scaling upper shelves
with ease for the most virgin of olive oils, elusive
jars of maraschino cherries. For a time in high school
I found movie magazines more enticing than mayonnaise.

I'd abandon my mother, sneak off to the glitzy aisle
for golden moments with Elvis, Marilyn, Marlon, Annette.
A double feature of Guilt and Regret. Soon,
I returned to heavenly Hellman's. I missed the lists.

Leaving home meant saying goodbye to Wegmans.
My destination: a small college town boasting one dull
market called Food Delight. That last summer morning I bid
farewell to my store, lingered in produce, wept

openly in the wondrous bakery, clutched my heart
by the Parmesan cheese. Mom gave me a gift
wrapped in a Wegmans flyer: all the grocery lists she'd saved,
next to each item my solid red check.

Roseland Park

Playground of the Finger Lakes

A flock of painted flamingos
glows fuchsia above the entrance gate.
The arcade beckons: a wooden pavilion
where Skee Ball reigns, and Madam Sonya—
inside a gilded cage—
doles out for a dainty dime
predictions for the coming week.

Her head swivels from side to side,
mesmerizes. Long lacquered nails
boast a Russian shade of red. I gaze
into heavy-lidded eyes, half expecting a wink,
an invitation to embrace her wild gypsy world.
If I bury my face in her saucy dress,
will the sequins reveal even more? I implore,
What does my future hold?

My parents escort me back into light.
Today is enough, they sigh. The sun
gleams like a yellow present,
a feast for here and now.
Popcorn perfumes the hot breeze.
Cotton candy tickles, turns my cheeks pink.

Snow-Bound Mannequins

Two barefoot blonde mannequins gaze
out of shop windows at white city streets.
Dressed in lush burgundy, designer hats—
they might be waiting for a bus,
wishing they'd worn warm socks or boots.

At thirteen, I wondered if mannequins
spoke when no one was looking,
complained about the pain of standing still,
pined for cheeseburgers and vanilla shakes.
I envied their clear skin, lacquered nails,
porcelain perfection.

When did I learn to savor the ways I could move
through life, tilt my chin toward the moon,
leave my footprints in silver snow?

Sweet Dreams, Dance Man

Once a chorus boy off-Broadway,
Jack sewed his own spangled shirts
in rented rooms ten dollars a night.
He bought the Starlight Express,
a studio squeezed—like big thighs into fishnets—
between Nate's Hots and the auto parts store.
Kids came in for tap and ballet.
Jack the Stitcher, parents called him,
when he whipped up costumes for shows.

Tricky sequins, flimsy fabrics,
glossy ribbon bowed to his skill.
He flossed with glitter thread.
Jack choreographed, shimmied, swayed,
shuffled off to Buffalo, no cramp roll
too wicked for his nimble feet.
Lithe legs withstood a middle-aged belly
stuffed with Snickers. *I march to my own cuisine,*
he said, eschewing greens. One week

before our spring recital, a heart attack
ended his Starlight run. Without insurance,
dear Jack ignored the pain.
His sister found him surrounded by needles—
the sewing kind—bald head peaceful
against a bolt of pink chiffon.
At the funeral Jack looked handsome

in a borrowed pin-striped suit,
his casket overflowing with candy bars

left by us, his dancers, who shimmered
near him in lavender lace.
We had never seen Jack so still.
In a daze, we waited
for his fingers to snap, alert us:
Places everyone, time to warm up.

Death of a Saleswoman

The tantalizing aroma of orange crullers
wafts from the gourmet bakery aisle in Sibley's,
our glitzy downtown emporium.

I work part-time in high school—in men's shirts,
pajamas, robes, underwear, ties. One Saturday,
a guy with stooped shoulders shuffles into the store.

I'm Joe, he says. *My wife died, I've lost weight.*
His clothes hang; he doesn't know his size.
How about a bathrobe? I ask, leading him

toward an ornate full-length mirror.
He tries on a crimson silk first, then a smart
blue plaid trimmed with gold cuffs.

Joe's body swims in a yellow dazzler
featuring deep pockets. That robe
makes both of us laugh. My supervisor

glares, her features mannequin-pale:
Your job is to sell, not schmooze.
The fashion play lasts way past lunch.

Joe's face picks up light. He starts to move
like Fred Astaire—a little stiff
but charming. My job on the line,

I send Joe off to the bakery, a whiff of Spring
in his step. He circles back with a glazed-
sugar smile, plus two orange crullers for me.

From a plastic hanger I remove a sleek, green
flannel robe, then a silver fleece
soft as a baby's cheek.

Sacristy of Sweets

I could not resist a good sugar cookie—
its scent a blessing—a wafer
much larger than the Body of Christ
Father Murphy held aloft at Sunday mass.
Mrs. Weger never mentioned
church at her bakery—her apron
sprinkled with holy dust

afloat on her wide frame. One slim
dollar bought you a path into heaven,
a dozen round angels arranged in a box,
paradise lined in wax paper.
I could ignore éclairs,
pass by pies, sacrifice doughnuts.
But a sugar cookie tempted sin—excess

calories forgiven with a sign of the cross.
Even now, when I hear a bell, I envision
Weger's Bakery on Thurston Road,
front door ajar on a sultry day. Trays
of confections beckon salvation.
Sugar crystals glisten like rosary beads.
Hail Mrs. Weger, full of grace.

Gift Shop on the Arctic Circle

Ice cold souvenirs cluster in frosted
window displays. Snow globes
flaunt their tinted geography of light
in this northern Norway town where
winter mist sparkles. My frozen toes

welcome extra pairs of woolen socks.
Hot coffee steams my blue tongue.
Never mind turning up the heat. Show me
auroral earrings in electric shades of green.
I'm never bored with the borealis.

Far from the maddening news, I use
my credit card to buy white silence,
at least a fur hat to muffle sound. Outside,
a painted sky reveals what noise conceals.

Sex and Utensils

Men fork, women spoon.
Consider the cannibal theory:
The utensil chooses the sex.

Fork is a poker all right,
with extra tines for meat,
less for lettuce and love.

Spoon curves like a swan's neck,
shining for that special hunk
when he will not be caught.

Is Knife only the awkward
referee, a fat blade twitching
between two fires?

Soliloquy

I find a candy wrapper
deep in the pocket
of a sweater destined for new adventures.
That wrinkled remnant
makes me pause.

Chocolate pleasure,
taste of another time—
our steps so light along the river path.
We planned a future
far beyond the Milky Way.

Where are you now, my sweet,
and are you also remembering?

12 Bright Oaks Drive

Glossy photos feature our family dwelling
of more than forty years. The couple who bought it
after my mother died gutted the inside,
turned home into chrome. I barely recognize the kitchen
where Mom and Auntie practiced magic in matching
aprons – gliding like Ginger Rogers and her twin
across the scuffed linoleum floor, whipping up casseroles
in well-worn cookware. The tin recipe box. Grandma Rose's
bell-shaped salt & pepper shakers. Sticky souvenir magnets
clinging to the refrigerator door. The lantern
light fixture swinging too low over the dinette table.
Who'd be first to lose a nose? We took bets.

My parents would be gobsmacked by the couture-chic
living room splattered on Zillow. No place
here for Dad's out-of-tune Hammond organ
bearing scratches from Buddy, our beloved cat.

Only the yard escaped. Dad is cutting our front lawn.
Skinny legs. Loose socks around his ankles
resemble horseshoes encircling a stake.
A red bandanna catches the sweat from his brow.
You look like a bank robber, Mom laughs from the porch—
above the din of the mower. She offers lemon meringue pie,
Genesee Cream Ale. Twilight, she settles on the faded
yellow sofa, an indentation in each section.
Hand on the cushion next to her, she beckons me

to her side. Together, we watch Dad finish his task.
Beneath the unrefurbished moon, nothing
beats the scent of fresh-mown grass.

Homage

for Richard

We piled into your vintage burgundy
'48 Chrysler each October, our fall
pilgrimage to the Finger Lakes for grape pies.
Oh, the Concord smell—the crust still warm.

Near dusk, we'd head home
as streaks of orchid purpled the sky.
Lilacs waited for us in front yards.

No one brought flowers to your funeral.
Picnic baskets lined the altar, the wild
aroma of grape pies rising.

In Place of Cake

We feast on wedding pies,
their round faces oozing rhubarb and peach
in the humid church reception hall.
The Greek caterer wields his knife like a kamikaze

confectioner's sword. When he raises
his arm to slice, we keep our hands
away from the pies—the risk of *finger food*
a distinct possibility.

Those desserts a delight, bland crusts
concealing jewels: rich berry colors,
chocolate cream, even a tart
lemon with its crown of singed meringue.

No one misses the traditional tower cake
frosted in paste. Pies offer choices;
guests relish the selections. Two long tables
soon empty. Square cardboard boxes

discarded in stacks look like the remains
of opened gifts. Off to one side, the bride glows
next to her handsome groom. Blind since birth,
he hears our exuberant praise of pies.

Behind his placid smile, a tapestry blooms
within: delicious blues, verdant greens,
musical forests of fuchsia and orange.

Dear Dad

Thirty years after your death
I bring a silver thermos of Manhattans
to Holy Sepulchre Cemetery on Dewey Ave.
Thirsty grass leans in a stiff breeze
off the lake. Marble markers
line up like bar stools.
In the hush of a summer afternoon
I toast your legacy. You savored

the joy of words, and the exhilarating ways
a stream of humor gurgled over ordinary stones.
Because of you, I imagine the world
as a succulent maraschino cherry
ripe with possibilities. Dad, you showed me
all of that shimmering energy.
I raise a glass to your light.
I touch my pen to the page.

The summer you died I found your wallet in your top drawer.
Driver's license, insurance, your secret recipe for window cleaner—
my pink and white Lady Bartender business card
with the slogan we agreed on: *I Mix Well.*

Thick brushstrokes garnish the menu

Purple Robe, Silver Swan

There are always flowers
for those who want to see them.
—Henri Matisse

A tree on its last limbs
holds court in the yard of my neighbor's row house.
Sue—in remission after chemo—
fills long days fashioning ornaments
to decorate this decrepit sentinel passers-by adore
at the corner of 28th Street and St. Paul.

Juggling a coffee mug and sketchbook on her front steps,
I start to draw the dangling charms. I'm no expert, yet
pushing pastel pencils across thick paper calms me.
Sue has added bouquets of teal bells. They crowd
a gold filigree butterfly. Panic sets in when I miss
the silver swan, then relief to spot it on another branch.

I can't bear any more loss.
Yellow mums comfort the lawn. I lower my mask,
sip my morning brew—adrift in this still life.

A short walk from Sue's finds Henri Matisse, my tonic of choice,
awake in our city's art museum, where I pledge allegiance
to his *Purple Robe and Anemones*. Sizzling yellows
mimic a honey bonfire amid turquoise and pink
in perfect sync with an exuberance of red.
A saucy woman flaunts a striped garment I covet.

Quarantined on the canvas, she stares at me from her neon space.
Blonde hair, beads, gutsy vibe—I half-expect a wink, a pep talk.
Blending with the anemones blazing in their wavy vase,
her purple energy a pulse so palpable
I want to jump rope beneath the glare of guards.

On the way home—my sketchbook blooming—
Sue perches on a stepladder in her small outdoor gallery.
She points at the tree. *We're survivors,* she says.
A new ornament hangs from a coffee-brown limb.
In the dim light I can't make out its shape.
Something with feathers.

The Society of Obscure Yellow Dresses

The Yellow Dress, Henri Matisse,
oil on canvas, 1929-31, Baltimore Museum of Art

Meets on Tuesdays at 9 am
at the Common Ground Espresso Bar in Hampden.
Usual spot—window table.

Feel free to join us—
if you are not *The Yellow Dress* by Matisse.
Full of itself, that dress. Gorgeous, yes.
Far from the only golden ticket in town.

We are the overlooked, sale-rack-markdowns, lost
delinquents who besmirch the yellow brand.
Amber, ochre, saffron, blond,
lutescent, never lily-livered.

We struggle to raise the hem of our self-esteem.
We try to shrink our distress.
We weep into our puffy sleeves.

We pay homage to Monsieur Matisse.
His skills rendered a masterpiece so fine
every other yellow dress in the world
pales in its luminous wake.

Paint us, too, we beg the artists passing by,
from our front table at Common Ground—
a quartet of lemons awash in lemon light.

Starry Night Diner

Behind the counter,
a scarry, scarry man
says *I learned to cook*
in Arles. He throws
daffodils on the grill
to flavor each palate
with flowers. Sun
light illuminates
his one good ear.

Bouquets of buttery
mashed potatoes
float like water lilies
on a blue plate
special. Tenderly,
the leafy green bridge
between peas and carrots
dissolves into mist.

Thick brushstrokes
garnish the menu.
I order a garden
salad with extra
yellow in praise of
Monet and Van Gogh.
My booth blurs
into a sailboat on the Seine.

Brush Strokes

I share a villa with Vincent
in the south of France.
First morning, I confide
after he shaves
his face feels like a flower
painted by Georgia O'Keeffe,
an artist not yet born.

I tell Van Gogh she plays
with frosting colors—mauve,
tangerine—made from a Santa Fe sky.
Vincent smiles, his lone ear
pale as a fallen petal.

Know what eclipses tangerine?
he says, gliding me toward the door
open to morning. The huge sun
a festive yellow blossom—a feast—
the light perfect without a hint
of stubble. I brush Vincent's cheek,
a tender canvas warm to my touch.

Goats in Wyman Park Dell

A chain gang with facial hair and horns
tames the steep sides of the grassy bowl

opposite the Baltimore Museum of Art.
Pungent goat permeates mild fall air.

Only a low electric fence separates me
from this battalion of bleaters.

Gathered here for a week, they spurn distance.
Foliage disappears on well-nibbled slopes.

Goaded by love, I release the billies and nannies,
guide them across the tree-lined street

to the museum's pillared front doors. Good news:
free admission for all. We skitter past

guards at the main desk who watch—wide-eyed—
my fragrant friends climb the staircase with ease.

I herd them toward mountain works. First, Cezanne's
Mont Sainte-Victoire Seen from the Bibémus Quarry.

For a few seconds they seem to relish the rising peak,
luminous contrast between blue sky, orange rock,

the savory temptation of green,
savvy patch of lavender with precipice.

Sassy creatures soon ignore my pleas, queue up near Matisse.
Pleasing bleats express rapture for the French master's

orgies of color and form. Goats recognize kin,
another wild beast. We browse in a field of time—

Still Life with Compote, Apples and Oranges.
We feast on the blissful promise of dessert.

The moon could use a little more sugar

Undaunted, We Dare to Swizzle

At the intersection of Tanqueray and tonic,
my poet friend laments a recent batch of rejections,
so I plan to create a Desolation Highball
laced with Campari—dark red, bitter.
Consider history. Doesn't a cocktail always show up?

I bet my gold necklace a guard slipped Anne Boleyn a Kir Royale
to ease the sword's blow. Did Noah stay sober on the Ark
with all that honking and bleating, the incessant roars?
Joy juice infuses paintings, too. I know Vermeer can't defend
himself, but that *Girl with a Pearl Earring* looks a tad tipsy.

People perpetually pick on Picasso, his fondness for absinthe.
No wonder he turned Blue. Liquor barons
named an espresso vodka after Van Gogh.
Bogie swilled gin in *The African Queen*. Whiskey sours
mixed in pitchers signaled the start of summer in our cul-de-sac.

I brought my mother to the Yardarm Tavern in Annapolis
the night my unwed sister gave birth to a baby girl.
Mom downed two Manhattans, fell asleep in my VW Bug.
For forty years, my father sang bass in a German choral group.
He loved Genesee Cream Ale, asked for a beer garden at his wake.

Intoxicating how words effervesce like music from a deep place.
I tucked a poem of mine inside Dad's casket—one
rejected by a journal the week before.

Accounting

Numbers startle my tongue.
20,000 pounds of ostrich feathers,
16,000 lemons
lost on the Titanic.
I picture all that fluff and fruit
carpeting the floor of the sea.
12 newly married couples
honeymooned on the ship. Every bride
survived. Only 1 groom.

In 6th grade, I wore a red plaid skirt
the night my brother sank in waves of dismay
at the county spelling bee.
He made it to the final 4.
Commentary, the word he missed.

Now, I'm adding up how long
my cousin Judy lived with Parkinson's.
It stole her speech, her sparkle,
the last ounce of air from her lungs.
16 years—my commentary reveals.
5,840 days.

Royal Dress Shop

Rochester, New York

Pruning the closet in my spare room,
I come across a summer dress
the color of coffee splashed with cream.
That shabby fabric takes me back to the '80s:
We pile into Auntie's trusty blue Buick—
Mom, Aunt Alvina, my sister Nancy, me—
fired up for a field trip to the Royal,
a fashion mecca on dicey North Clinton Ave.
Once inside we swoon in unison, swarm

metal racks swollen with stylish creations.
Four dressing rooms beckon, one for each of us.
A spirit of play infuses our day. We shut out the world.
Mom serenades her old girdle. Auntie gushes over a gold
polyester pantsuit with a plunging neckline.
My sister parades her chic attitude. I crave sequins,
ruffles, girly clothes. The well-coiffed owner
offers blackcurrant tea in ceramic cups.
She serves brownies on neon paper plates.

We load our loot into the car's cavernous trunk—
new frocks hidden from Dad's woeful eyes until
past happy hour. They're gone now. Mom, Dad, Auntie.
Nancy died young. Even the Buick expired.
The Royal Dress Shop disappeared in a flash

after the landlord doubled the rent.
I cling to this light brown garment with eyelet trim,
frilly collar. In its flowery skirt, stories bloom.

Cubicle 4

Dead Salmon? Rotten Raspberry?
No comfort radiates from these pink walls
in the Breast Imaging Center's waiting room.
I survey my sisters—faces beyond pale—
all of us called back for further testing.

Someone half-shouts my name, brings me to Cubicle 4,
possible setting for a Stanley Kubrick film—
less *Lolita*, more *A Space Odyssey.* I remove
sweater and bra, don a paper cape,
wait for take off. Sweat soaks my brow.

Cheryl, robot clone, escorts me across the hall.
A foreign machine—HAL 9000?— compresses my breast.
I'm halfway to Jupiter now. A quick trek
back to Cubicle 4. More waiting.

Kim leads me to the sonogram outpost
where aliens lurk behind ceiling tiles.
The radiologist pops in, a vision in astral white.
You're fine, she says. *Several benign cysts.*
See you in one year. Music cue: "The Blue Danube."

Cubicle 4 surrenders my earth clothes.
Struck by starlight, I return in triumph
to the galactic splendor of Pink.

Dressing Room

> Valentina Orellana-Peralta, 14, died in her mother's arms on 12/23/21 in a Burlington clothing store, after an LAPD officer opened fire on an unarmed suspect, and one bullet pierced the dressing room wall. Valentina was shopping for a dress for her quinceañera.

Growing up, I spent hours in dressing rooms
not much larger than an upright coffin,
lined with hooks and distorted mirrors—
my mother and I in such close proximity
the space felt like a birthing place.
Every zipper resembled an umbilical cord
I longed to slice in two.

Buried under a cluster of plaid skirts,
ugly corduroy pants—I ached for fresh air.
Holiday sales or back-to-school bargains
signaled dread. It wasn't all torture.
Mom's agony while squirming into
stiff girdles and voluminous brassieres
stirred laughing fits I could not suppress.

Hold these pins, she'd say
as I doubled over, spilling my M&M's.
Sometimes we both dissolved in giggles.
Prom time called for battle tactics,
Mom fighting off the billowing crinolines,

eyeing bust and hem before the price tag.
She earned her corsage.

Looking back, I recognize the miracle—
how my mother and I emerged alive
from a thousand dressing rooms, how we walked
together into the safe burst of afternoon light.

At Mac's Drive-In

Between Waterloo and Geneva in upstate New York,
a red sign boasts RICHardson Root Beer—
bold caps crowning a seasonal, shabby-chic
fast food joint called Mac's Drive-In.

On April visits home, my brother and I
drove to Mac's for opening day.
Free root beer flowed in frothy streams.
Side-by-side on spinning chrome stools,

we inhaled the menu's endless list of possibilities:
succulent fries, onion rings like battered jewels,
rows of sizzling red hot dogs
posing as butterflies glued to the grill.

Richard, I felt closest to you
on those delicious trips to Mac's,
your vintage Chrysler humming.
You died on the first Monday of January

after a brief illness. Stubborn man, you refused
all my calls. You'll miss Mac's opening this Spring—
its sixtieth season—close to the years
you lived in this world.

You didn't want flowers, but I'll save the stool
next to mine—say everything I once held back.
Never mind if it looks like I'm talking
to myself. In your honor

I will order two Hoffman's All Beef Red Hots.
A cascade of ketchup. Skip the relish.
Overhead, puffy clouds on a platter,
shaped like swirls of soft ice cream.

A Treat for Joseph

My grandfather talked to his scarecrow
in the fields near Dundee.
He called it *Joseph.*

Evenings after supper, pie
warm in our bellies,
he would sneak an extra slice

as we rushed out the back door.
A treat for Joseph, Grandpa said,
the pastry a jewel purpling his palm.

Is it really for the crows? I asked,
when the first frost
bit through the withered corn,

my words sticking together
in a child's singsong way,
my hand lost in his.

Grandpa's breath slowed, his lungs
a sudden burden.
His voice no longer worked.

The last light surrendered. We watched
the fresh-baked moon
comfort layers of autumn sky.

The Cure

Because my heart hung low in my chest,
a dull lump barely beating,
my parents summoned me home. I spent
that summer in rehab in our backyard.
For days I faced a taunting sun, lost
myself in murder mysteries—each corpse
a new best friend. Mom stirred tonics,
pink and tart. Dad turned the garden

hose into a wild cowboy lasso.
He watered me, along with the plants,
until my earrings sounded like chimes.
Serenaded by a lawnmower symphony,
my parents discharged me.
And what of your hurt, Dad asked,
his words not so much a question. Rather,
a tender light for my passage.

Keeper of the Moon

for Ken and Helen

Monhegan Island, off the coast of Maine.
Orange and purple swirls
paint a sherbet sunset treat,
dessert at the end of day.

These colors conjure you, except
you'd pass up sherbet
for a double scoop of nonfat ice cream.
You slipped away so fast.

I take comfort in your new role
mixing night sky confections,
no one better to flavor the stars.
The moon could use a little more sugar.

The lighthouse blinks our secret code.
How I miss the way you held me.

Breathe

Air: entrée and dessert.
Sweet Air. Savory Air.

Each inhalation thrills.
I am greedy for Air.

My sister became a warrior—
an oxygen tank her armor,

her silver camouflage. She died
four days after Christmas

fighting for one more,
one more breath.

Silent Air. Holy Air.
I sign my name with Air.

Breathe in, I tell myself.
Make a fist with Air.

Homeless Man Outside Walgreens

Baltimore, MD

The day before the blizzard
he sits cross-legged on cold concrete
next to a trash can, a gray
blanket loose around his shoulders.

He holds up a homemade sign. Wait,
he doesn't have a home.
I give him a dollar and a smile.
Thanks, angel, he says.

Sir, if I were an angel
I'd whisk you off to a Greek
Paradise where gray is banned.
Instead, we find this diner that serves
breakfast all day. Over pancakes,

we talk about city life. You call
Freddie Gray your brother, never mind
the different shades of your skin.
You are kin, in the unruly way
layers of circumstance pile up

like a thousand gray blankets. Change
begins one exchange at a time.
We signal for the waitress
to refill our coffee cups.

Bobby

Ambassador Hotel, Los Angeles
June 5, 1968

The aftermath of stirring victory
turns to grief in a kitchen passage.
A bullet ruins his brain just past midnight.
He dies the next day.

On the East coast, that same fatal shot
tears my 21st birthday
into fragments. Metallic
taste in place of cake.

A proud idealist,
I cherish Robert Francis Kennedy—
campaigned for him,
met him twice.

My mother wakes me early.
For months I'd waited
for this turning point.
Instead of birthday greetings

I hear bad news.
My sorrow the bitter length of a funeral train.
21 means I can vote.
Does it matter now?

In the hotel chaos, Ethel
offers her husband comfort.
I'm with you, she whispers.
She is 40 and pregnant. He is 42.

After Another School Shooting

in memory of Uvalde, May 24, 2022

Who could bear to leave a son or daughter here
in this cemetery after the final prayer?
Makeshift markers rest like forgotten toys

left out in the rain. Trees in green skirts
become mothers for a time.
Listen to the lullaby of leaves in evening light.

The miracle of sleep lies in waking up,
bedsheets tossed aside, a scramble to brush teeth,
rush downstairs for burnt toast and blue backpacks,

quick kisses, the litany of noisy goodbyes.
See the school bus: a lemon limousine.
In the distance, a black hearse looms.

Where are all the stuttered words, silly songs?
A chorus of cherished voices forever asleep
beneath a blanket of teddy bears.

The Sounds of Sorrow

Maybe one of the reasons we are alive
is to hold each other's sorrow—Ross Gay

Posters of our mascot, Sammy Snake, spruced up
the bland walls of our speech therapy rooms.

His playful features in cartoon colors
reminded children how to say *s-s-s.*

Chuck Irvin and I bonded at weekly
speech meetings, where we teased each other

with our best Sammy impressions.
S-s-see you next time, he always said.

Our connection deepened after Chuck revealed his illness,
the disastrous plague afflicting gay men in the '80s,

early '90s. During late-night conversations
our phone cords hung in heavy coils. Sometimes

we spoke in syllables, gentle murmurings.
I'm so scared, he whispered.

The Supremes revived him. Diana Ross,
her sweet, smoky soprano close to a cure.

Speech friends rallied. Curled up on Chuck's mottled
brown sofa, we watched videos of the Supremes,

glamorous girls in white feather boas that snaked
around their waists. We swayed and sang along:

"Stop! In the Name of Love"—tossing out our best
Sammy hiss, squeezing Chuck's hand.

Only thirty-nine, he succumbed in March, 1993,
surrounded by his parents, his sister,

his steadfast Dalmatians. That summer six of us
gathered at Chuck's gravesite, our solemn faces

mirrors of grief. We reminisced about Sammy Snake—
who offered s-s-solace, taught us lessons about shedding,

the art of letting go. Raising a sparkling toast to Chuck,
we mustered a sassy chorus of "Someday We'll Be Together."

Emily Dickinson & Cher Settle In for a Heart-to-Heart

They slip from separate eras into a booth at the Homestead Café,
sip blackcurrant tea. Cher's voluminous, white feather boa
brushes the floor as Emily confides, *I'm writing a verse about Hope.*
In the slanted light of a late winter afternoon,
Cher's cleavage contrasts with Emily's high-necked blouse,
yet the mega-stars relax in each other's thoughtful gaze.

Cher unearths Calvin Klein perfume from her faux leopard bag,
dabs Eternity behind her ears. Emily's skin glows—
a pale miracle free of blush. She whispers:
Behind Me—dips Eternity
Before Me—Immortality
Myself—the Term between—
Their laughter resonates. Cher's lacquered nails pat Emily's wrist.
I get you, Babe, she coos.

My sister, Nancy, sang Cher's songs. She played a toy mandolin,
carried it around like a pet. Younger, always breaking things—
my birthday statue of the Virgin Mary, all my best perfume bottles:
Tabu, Moonlight Mist (the spray). Later, she redeemed
herself, taught me how to use a tampon & flirt with panache.
Nancy praised my poems. A bundle of maladies took her fast,
not before she sang her own song, *I love you. I am not afraid.*

Emily & Cher, timeless in the Homestead Café—
Death but the Drift of Eastern Gray.

Jean and Alvina

A pair of permed heads, a team
in green and red matching sweaters,
my mother and aunt raked leaves
into impressive hills. Their knitted gloves
discouraged blisters. They laughed
even when the wind played games,
adding leaves to spaces already cleared.
Evenings after dinner—my dad long dead—
Mom and Auntie washed dishes: a duo
in sync, whispering leftover gossip
that swirled like graffiti down the kitchen drain.
A game of cards, one Manhattan each,

they thrived on friendship.
So different from their childhood
when family illness parted them. Mom
lived in an orphanage for years.
She seldom talked about the past,
only of holes in her shoes. Auntie
stayed with kin in another town.
Blisters of the heart. The sisters
never lost each other again,
until Aunt Alvina died at ninety-five.
Mom would sit alone on her window seat,
watching autumn leaves.

Manet's The Dead Toreador

—oil on canvas, 1864
in memory of David Simpson

Dressed in finery, the fallen toreador
might be asleep—face placid, eyes closed—
save for a small pool of red
visible beneath his left shoulder blade.
The bullfighter's silvery stockings
remain intact, his sash unstained.

Among the gallery's scenic treasures
The Dead Toreador resonates most.
I keep returning to his horizontal form,
jet-black suit, alabaster shirt, the sword
wrapped in a muleta of ancient rose.
My gaze lingers on the splash of red.

Next morning, a message relays
my poet-friend's death from ALS.
Brave warrior, he dared to wave red
in the face of a fatal disease. Blind since birth,
he moved with a toreador's grace,
his life a masterpiece filled with music and wit.

Once, at a poetry workshop in Cape May,
the power went out during happy hour.
Leaving behind our Manhattans, Dave led me

from the hotel lounge back to my room.
He was my light, my guide.
Before he died, he told a nurse, *I believe in love.*

I want to emblazon those words in red
on a cape I wear into the world.

Elegy with Squeegee Boys

A trio of city teens cool in denim and high-tops
swarms my Honda at a red light.
Armed with spray bottles, a slew of washcloths,
the kids create a cascade of water across my dusty windshield.
Would they scorn the nun's prayer I saw on Facebook?
I am touched by effervescent showers of Joy
flowing down over me from the Invisible.
Spring water quenches my thirst. Thoughts ripple December chill.

Terence Hickey, the boy I loved in second grade,
drowned in the Genesee River. Fishing with older boys
he lost his footing, fell from their boat into cold,
olive water. My dad brought me to say goodbye.
This eight-year-old angel asleep in a satin-lined box,
pale in his white First Communion suit.
I begged him to open his eyes.
Holding Dad's hand, I took in Terry's features—
the cascade of blond curls adrift on his forehead,
freckled nose, the crescent scar an indentation on his right cheek.
Thanks to my father I keep Terry's face
like the memory of a rare flower's brief reign.

St. Mary's. The hush of hospital hallways after dark.
For two nights before he died, my dad asked me to keep
a cool washcloth on his forehead. Every twenty minutes,
although I'm sure the clocks had stopped,
I repeated the ritual: remove the warm cloth, rinse, replace.

Studying my father's face—the widow's peak, the fine straight nose,
exquisite eyebrows—I probably babbled nonstop. Dad murmured
syllables of gratitude, his breath the last notes of some old song.

Rolling down my squeaky-clean window, I thank the squeegee boys,
hand the tall one a few timeworn bills. Above his mask,
large eyes smile—such a rich earth-toned brown.
His lashes extra long.
The traffic light turns green, almost effervescent,
three shades brighter than the Genesee.

After Forty-Seven Years I Remember the Cornish Hens

June, 1977

The forlorn scent of dying roses
drifts from their messy beds.
A pair of Cornish hens—patted dry—
sits in the sink waiting for a chance
to sizzle in the pan. Everything happens
in the kitchen and the yard.
We named the dog Pepper. Sometimes
a good sneeze is the only way to release
sudden shocks that knock us down.
In the photo, I wear a crown of wire curlers
and try to smile—Pepper's face a sunbeam,
my eyes missing light. On the wall calendar
purple gemstones glimmer over a square—
June 5th, my 30th birthday—not enough space
to disclose the dual events of that date.
How they reverberated, what they cost.

I'm sorry, he said, *I can't marry you.*
I felt a hurricane throttle my throat.
The ring seared my finger.
Maybe I touched his mustache, a minus sign
above his trembling mouth,
the taste of sorrow a lost shade of pearl.

Heat filled the kitchen. The Cornish hens
turned tough and crisp. Minutes passed.

How long does it take for a heart to burn?
The phone rang and rang, my mother
calling from upstate New York.
Your father...can you come home?
I could barely hear her voice
collapsing like a broken star.

Endless Feast

In a desk drawer I find an envelope
marked with my childish scrawl:
Toby's hair. Inside, a black and white curl
clipped from our neighbor's springer spaniel.

Summer mornings my brother and I sprinted
up Margaret Street to the turquoise house,
Toby's tongue a sloppy love greeting.
We played together in dappled sunlight—
my giddy sibling, Toby, me.

What we lose reminds us
we don't always know
what will matter later on.

Time, a feast, a Frisbee
tossed into youth's bone-white days.
Time, a tease, a leash
never long enough.

Limburger – a fragrance fierce as love

Kaleidoscope

after Hikmet

I never knew I liked white space,
the air between words, between lines.
What worlds will I build in the snow?

I didn't know how much I loved questions.
Did you ever ask yourself: *How will I tell my stories?*

Wallace Stevens rode over Connecticut in a glass coach.
Not my style. Behind the wheel of my vintage green Checker taxi—
the meter off—I'm ready for a scavenger hunt.
Come with me, this late winter light so full of promise.

Kindergarten: Every day I brought to school
a tan paper shopping bag filled with toys,
in case the teacher ran out of things to do.
Will my name always spell *sassy?*

I began with color:
Grandma Alice gave me a kaleidoscope—
a universe of sparkles on my fifth birthday.
Didn't know how much I liked
Jell-O, the way its sequin colors tremble and glow.
Black Cherry, Strawberry, Lime.

Houses and rooms are full of perfumes, Walt Whitman said.
I never knew I loved straw-colored Limburger cheese,

my father's favorite feast. I hid in the attic
to escape the fumes. After he died,
I missed the pungent aroma.
Limburger—a fragrance fierce as love.
                                        I can't lasso enough "L" words.

                                        Lemons: 16,000 sank
                                        inside the Titanic April 15, 1912.
                                        Sour. A partner to Sorrow?

Lingerie: A slip, a silk robe, a gold brassiere.
A rose, a rose, a rose.
Can a flower hear with petals that look like ears?

I didn't know how much I loved Van Gogh.
He lost an ear, sold only one painting in his lifetime.

Vincent, that last afternoon in Auvers
the sun pays you homage, blooms
lemon-gold at your wake.
Night arrives broken, until
a new amber light pulsates in the sky.
Does death makes you a star?

I can hear a star
                    from afar, the light
                                        years of language.

Martin Buber spoke the language of philosophy.
Play is the exultation of the possible, he said.

I wonder if he felt an I-Thou connection to M&M's?
Maybe he smuggled those delectable buttons
into Jerusalem—a playful caravan of colorful confections.
Red, Violet, Orange.
Martin&Me, pro-vibrant.

> Mars Confectionery introduced M&M's
> September 10, 1941. First candy to travel
> into space. Chocolate astronauts?

Play the M&M game with me:
Mice&Men, Mars&Moon.
Myth&Metaphor,
Melon&Melancholy.

I loved a man who spoke only the language of Home Depot.
Never knew before, but I discover
my passion for that store runs deep.
Circling the lot in my green Checker taxi,
my eyes try to find a parking space marked "Reserved for Grief."
I ask a helpful clerk for tools to cope with loss.
Perhaps a power saw, wire cutters, a hymnal of nails?

She points upward, toward signs hanging from heaven.
Paint, she says, her voice a solace in the lumber-dust air.
Lining the paint aisle, sample color cards
in a literature of neons, a litany of pastels, a tender
lamentation of neutrals.

Who knew my healing would begin in Home Depot?
Beside me, on the passenger seat of my jewel-green vehicle,
this palette of words, this gush of colors:
Lantern Light, North Star, Plum.
I turn on the taxi's meter—my *Iced Green Apple* taxi—
and give myself a destination. *Lilac Promise, After the Rain.*

Hymn to Myself

I am a blooming encyclopedia of effervescent knowledge,
I text my friend Wendy who offered exuberant praise
of the restaurant I high-fived.
Glowing, I describe my own poetry
in a recent online journal. I gluttonize
on adjectives. Never mind what experts say.

Brought up in the Catholic faith where nuns
favored humility, I would cast my eyes
downward at the slightest compliment. Now,
I can't get enough of myself.
And why not? Walt Whitman eased me
onto the path. His luminous ode to the individual.

Mary Oliver—steeped in wisdom—advised
announcing your place in the family of things.
To that end, I bought a megaphone. How's this
for a miracle? I'm not assigning ten stars
to me alone. I'm planting kisses on my friends,
even the vagabond with the cup at the curb.

Although it's not Sunday, I am singing a hymn.
Let all the brazen Hallelujahs multiply
like loaves. Let our gifts—yours and mine—glow
in the resplendent light that makes all of us beautiful

Even the green Spanish olives lighten up

Goddess of Swizzle

Two stirring weeks
at the Maryland Bartending Academy
earn me an MBA. A perfect score
tops off my final test—concocting
twenty drinks in less than ten minutes.
The huge clock behind the bar
keeps time with swizzle sticks.
Drunk with success, I find
a job at a waterfront dive
called Captain Clyde's. Late in the day,
men saunter in from skipjacks,
plop down on stools, order lemonade pie
and beer. Beer! The Goddess of Mixology
pours suds into deep blue steins. I long

for an occasion to slice limes
into neat wedges, pluck
a maraschino cherry from its ruby cage.
Past sunset, aquamarine lights
glow in the mammoth jukebox.
Couples dance on dark brown carpet
that bunches up like walrus hide.
Mellow with hops, the oystermen
sing their chanteys. Even the moon
tunes in—a gleaming white coaster.
I forget about Manhattans,
Pomegranate Martinis, Side Cars.

Stars like specks of beer foam
spatter the perfect night sky.

Cocktails with the Queen

in memory of Queen Elizabeth II and Prince Philip

In her sitting room, Queen Elizabeth and I
welcome the tray balanced with snifters
of Dubonnet, gin, lemon slices, small
floes of ice. We clink glasses, toast the royals,
gossip over juicy news: Brexit-this, Harry-that.
The Dubonnet glows ruby in London light.

After lunch, the queen summons a leash.
We walk her dogs. Stunning in a yellow primrose
Hermès headscarf, she pats my arm, proclaims:
If I wore beige, no one would know me. Later on,
at a palace affair for a well-medaled duke,
the monarch carries her sartorial signature—

a classic black Launer handbag, suede-lined.
She loans me a regal patent leather purse. No pause
to nap or recover from painstaking research
for my blockbuster, "A Day in the Life of the Queen."
Her Majesty snaps me out of my trance.
We don purple coats, matching hats.

A carriage awaits. Perhaps a prince.
I scrawl in my notebook—*Dinner with Phil.*

Celestial Nightmare

Imagine a computer running the moon:
a major malfunction scrambles her phases.

Lunar parts wax and wane
at whim, giving way

to a lopsided crescent, a broken gibbous,
a full girl unsure of herself.

Fix-it guys take space elevators
right to the moon's back door.

High on Milky Ways, they muck up
a galaxy of repairs. Earth suffers—

tides fizzle, menstrual cycles disappear,
dogs forget to bay. Moon goes

home with the geeks,
riding a see-through elevator

down to their pick-up trucks
where the right tools await. Poor moon,

her face needs more light.
She's lost her pearly tint.

Don't mess with my moon, you lunatics.
Put her back in the sky.

My Prince of Cheese

for Ron Fader

My cheese man wears marigold shirts,
sings like a dairy canary.
His kingdom, a circular display
at Eddie's on St. Paul Street.
As soon as I enter the market, he's waiting
with a grin and a Gruyère.
He tries to be fair, but we both know
he favors luscious provolone,
mozzarella, Savello di Roma—
flavors of Italy's boot in every bite.

Oh, how gingerly he cradles
each small package of perfection:
flaxen wedges wrapped in cellophane.
When Ron says *Cheese*,
shoppers click their heels, then buy.
Cow, goat, and sheep visions
curdle in his eyes. He weeps with joy.
To think I might have passed him by.
My prince reeks of cheer, his taste buds
a bouquet, a gourmet blossom.

Picture us together, a pair of Camembert
connoisseurs. On Sundays, we tone it down,
make lasagna madly, our pajamas
dotted with Parmesan.

Ballet and Mushrooms

My cousin's text message skewers
her vacation plans. Thank you, AutoCorrect.
I'm sure Fran meant *ballet and museums*—
favorite pastimes in Santa Fe. Still,
my mind conjures a cluster of fleshy
ballerinas alert in sheer Shiitake-shaped
tutus, pirouetting across the cave-dark stage
like appetizers in motion.

Beware the denouement.
A pair of Deathcaps among the corps de ballet
catches the principal male dancer unaware.
After a shaky jetė, he collapses—
in a tumult of tights—into the pit.

Even in my fungal state,
I'm gobsmacked by diction,
how the perfect word in a poem
rises en pointe.

Twist

Come on, baby, he cajoled us.
Chubby Checker changed history,
challenged our pelvises, much like Elvis.
Only Chubby made it seem easy,
his jovial face living proof we could groove
despite warnings from our chiropractors
to abandon this ludicrous dance.

In the lounge's dim light, you request
a Bombay Martini with a twist.
I picture the lemon remnant gyrating
round and round this slippery cocktail glass.
It startles the laid-back gin, wins
applause from the bar's docile limes,
thrills obese maraschino cherries.
Even the green Spanish olives lighten up.

Their red pimiento beacons pulse—
Come on, let's twist again—
like the buzzer at the bistro
that says your table's ready.

It Had to Be Good to Get Where It Is

Coca-Cola slogan, 1926

Esteemed Brain Tonic and Intellectual Beverage,
John Pemberton called it, after he cooked up
the first batch—perfect remedy for hangovers,
headaches. Later, a reputation as a laundry helper,
rust remover, ham glaze. Like Jell-O's inventor,
he sold off his interest, moved on. I sip a concoction

sure to stimulate my sugar-hungry brain,
escalate my IQ to genius. Oh, Mr. Pemberton,
if not for your backyard fire, I might be wallowing
in chilled herbal tea, sinking in a sea of lemonade.
Or worse, a Kool-Aid addict hiding packets
of fruity contraband inside self-help magazines,

satisfying my habit at midnight beneath
a Coca-Cola sky. Mr. Pemberton, I sing your name.
So what if you relinquished your share. You're the man
who paired coca leaves with extract of kola nut.
Elixir Entrepreneur, Inventor of Potion Number One.
To get where you are, you had to be good.

A Farewell to Cool Whip

O cumulus cloud in a cup,
luscious frothy cream
lathering my lemon pie.

I wallow in your whiteness,
so airy on my spoon,
the way you coat my throat—

tenderize my tongue. One quick lick,
I swoon. Halo-light in my fridge
beside the dark jar of peanut butter.

Too bad your ingredients
filibuster in my veins: *high fructose*
corn syrup, polysorbate 60. All

that *guar gum* can't be good.
Hydrogenated vegetable oil
spells Gallbladder Tease.

I want to believe you are spun
from the pure armpits of angels, yet
my nutritionist has ordered you out, out.

Goodnight, Sweet Decadence.
Rest well in your plastic trash can tomb.

My Gig as Tinsel and Beau

Christmas, 1982

Inside this claustrophobic reindeer house, I practice
playing with the handles—turning moves the heads,
squeezing opens and closes the reindeer mouths.
One lone peephole showcases the children's
expectant faces. I speak in festive voices:
baritone for Beau, high-pitched for Tinsel.

My caribou couple poses in front of the snow-
frosted hut near the café at the old Hutzler's store.
The scent of hot chocolate drifts. I long for a cup.
First night on the job, the little microphone
spews raspy sounds. Beau's handle sticks.
Blisters form. My tapered seat induces
an onset of holiday hemorrhoids.

A girl named Teresa introduces herself as five.
I want you to sing with me, Tinsel and Beau:
Jesus Loves Me, Jee-sus, Dear Jesus My Lord.
She bellows the hymn—a Bette Midler mimic.
Reindeer Training School bans any mention
of religion. My antler pressure rises.

I don't dare pray. Tinsel and Beau save the day.
They hum along to the Jesus hymn. Looking back
on my minimum-wage Talking Reindeer stint,
no other job has ever measured up. I learned

how to comfort with a big reindeer heart,
and when I couldn't sing the words
I figured out a way to hum.

The Center for Useless Splendor

My neighbor, Pat, gave me an eggplant hat,
purple and green, made of felt.
A three-inch stem pokes up from the top.

As soon as I lower the cloche over my curls
I become an invincible vegetable goddess
ready to face shadows, sorrow,

the challenge of mid-winter dark. Pat says
she found my hat at the Farmer's Market.
I suspect she succumbed

to the sales rack at that shop in Fells Point—
The Center for Useless Splendor.
Regulars ignore the main floor,

despite the sequins peppering the parquet.
Savvy customers choose the basement
where party lights glimmer

beneath a turquoise chandelier. Rare
artifacts line shelves. On a velvet divan,
silver seashells play saxophone duets.

Mermaid mannequins flaunt
shimmery lingerie, and fruit-shaped handbags
shudder with crystal embellishments.

Why not an eggplant hat? Especially in December.
A jewel of its kind sharing space
with a radish, rhubarb, a riot of rutabaga.

Urban Happy Hour

Kids open a fire hydrant
in our neighborhood one summer night.
Strawberry Kool-Aid gushes out. At first
we think it might be rust or blood,
all of us delirious from too much news.

Patsy Krugel fetches a pitcher and glasses
from her pink kitchen. We toast
the end of a hot day until
city workers stop our fun,
close our surreal refreshment stand.

Traces of red
still visible in the street, Mrs. Krugel
in her 80s and full of learning
tells it this way: *anything can happen*
along the path of a zipper.

Pat's Dancing School

On Brooks Avenue, I drive by a boarded-up
eyesore the size of an extra-large chicken coop.
This abandoned shack once housed
all the sparkling confetti of my girlhood.
My mind ricochets to 1957. I see Miss Pat,
a dark-haired pixie with legs the length of the Finger Lakes,
her limbs a vision in black fishnet hose.
On a raised platform inside the front door—

puffing on a filtered Pall Mall—
she purses her scarlet lips then stuffs
our parents' cash into a silvery drawstring bag.
Lemon breath mints freckle the lacquered desk.
I salivate over Miss Pat's neon manicured nails,
shiny as the metal plates on her patent leather heels.
Scrambling into my own worn tap shoes, I greet
my peers. Gangly and loose, six of us face the mirrored

wall in the small back room, waiting for the music.
A 45 spins on a blue player. Miss Pat,
Goddess of Iridescence, sizzles in sequins
as she sweet-talks commands:
Toe Tap
                    Ball Heel
                                        Brush Drag
                    Shuffle

I thrived in that crowded closeness,
Miss Pat's sultry perfume wafting over our heads
as we tapped our simple Morse codes.
Fluorescent lighting the only fake thing.
Before recitals, satin and lace costumes emerged
from bags stored in a tiny closet. Glitter
dotted the floor like ants decked out for Mardi Gras.
Sometimes a mouse popped up from its tutu netting bed.

The place glistened with possibilities, unlike
my gray grammar school just down the block,
where nuns in black habits tapped
rulers against our desks, scolded us in pale tones.
Pat's Dancing School expanded the rooms
in my brain into a glamorous rapture.
I felt forever draped in layers of chiffon,
ready to face the worlds I didn't know,

Miss Pat's voice a constant refrain:
Give me a dance, girls. Raise those chins.
Smile from the inside, or the music won't work.

You Are a Peach

A tiny woman, delicate in a blue cotton dress,
stands leaning on a cane in front of her house
near the Piazza del Mercado. Beneath a frizz of white hair

her face speaks: brown from years in the Italian sun.
Age spots on her forehead like dabs of chocolate. Eyes that grin
with the glee of a rascal. In her smile, the joy of a beautiful life.

I am...a...prune, she says, gazing at me, her English hesitant.
I search for the right words in her language. It's the summer
I spend two weeks in Italy studying poetry.

Sei una pesca, I manage to affirm, touching the fuzz on her arm.
We both laugh and share the morning. The sun
a velvet globe aglow in the orchard of the sky.

Billy and Clarie, the Alligator and the Wig

Uncle Billy built an airplane in the garage
he called the *luh bor' a to ry*—although,
legally blind, he had lost his license to fly.
Aunt Clarie grew hibiscus that shimmered
like pink-petaled lollipops. She whipped up
gourmet treats, a baking sheet her silver wand.

One summer I stayed at their Florida home
on a lake ruled by a black alligator
they named Orange Julius. An eccentric
neighbor, Miss Lily, willed her gewgaws to locals.
At her help-yourself wake, Billy and Clarie
chose a giant pickle dish, a stack of scarves,

two pairs of pigskin gloves. Billy elbowed me
toward a fluffy yellow wig with a rhinestone
barrette. *Play is the mother of fun*, he said.
After Clarie died, Billy kept her ashes
inside a prized cookie tin he garnished
with a fresh hibiscus each day. Orange Julius

disappeared. In dreams, Billy flies his plane
above the Magic Kingdom. His vision clear,
he wears leather gloves, an olive paisley scarf.
Forever by his side, Clarie holds a pickle dish
loaded with fudge, while Orange Julius,
now a blond, glitters near the lake.

Kitchen Couture

My mother and aunt dolled up
in Alfred Dunner. His drip-dries
transformed them
into chefs, they claimed—
flavored the meat loaf, fortified
the cheese soufflé.
Paisley rejuvenates, my aunt gushed,
posing with an onion in her palm.

My mother abandoned aprons,
her Dunner pants a coat of armor
repelling spills and stains.
The sisters sliced and diced in Dunner
beneath their curly perms. Thanksgiving,
when my aunt wore her peacock blouse,
our turkey emerged from the oven a triumph—
both birds vying for praise.

Yesterday, the neon Dunner sign
took me back to McCurdy's in upstate New York:
two ladies traipse into a dressing room
hoisting twenty pounds of clothes. Shoes off,
girdles hiked up, they choose what fits, what's hot,
what goes with dinner, and Alfred Dunner.
I'm the kid in a chair, at peace with pins
and polyester, dreaming about dessert.

Watching Law & Order with Ted and Rezsin

We climbed three flights of stairs to the top floor
on Chestnut Street, changed into pj's,
watched *Law & Order* on the black and white TV—
rabbit ears askew. No amount of murder
or gore distracted from the sweet reassurance
of this ritual with my Albany kin, savoring
our favorite show shoulder-to-shoulder
in Ted and Rezsin's old double bed.

During commercials, we chatted about our day:
Rezsin baking lasagna casseroles
for the latest Save the Pinebush community feast,
Ted recalling the poets I'd read aloud to him.
You even sound like Billy Collins, he said one
rainy afternoon when I'd finished my rendering
of "Fishing on the Susquehanna in July."

Despite failing eyesight, Ted—head crowned
with angelic wisps of white hair—always
recognized Jerry Orbach onscreen,
his Detective Lennie Briscoe suave in a tan
trench coat, richly toned voice a balm.
We half-expected Jerry to turn back
into El Gallo, his famed role in *The Fantasticks*,
and render the signature song...*if you remember,*
then follow. Follow, follow, follow, follow.

Even now, when *Law & Order*
comes on—a dead body, a bloody knife—
I feel that same comfort like a scarf
made of moonlight and tender stars.
It's easy to remember Rezsin
call out as I headed back to my room
filled with antiques and books:
If you're cold, honey,
there's an extra blanket
right on top of the pinball machine.

Alligator at Walmart

Through plate glass I see a dark form
ooze her way toward Walmart.

Her destination—handbags, a smug
glance at the competition? Or housewares:
scales on sale, a Swiffer for the tail?

Mrs. Gator's excursion abruptly
curtailed by unfriendly doors—

the automatic kind. She heads home,
no doubt relieved by a good excuse
not to patronize this monstrous warehouse

where bargains beckon like quicksand.
I spend hours roaming a maze of aisles.

The long check-out line leaves me cold,
weighed down with plastic bags,
my limbs stiff as logs.

I'd rather romp with the reptiles
in Alligator Lagoon, one eye

visible above the surface,
hungry for a stray shopping cart,
leg of cashier, Armageddon.

Before the Last Chapter

I am wintering with Stephen King.
His lengthening shadow and eerie words
frighten the birds at my feeder.
Still, my fingers relish suspense.
They press into every snow-white page

as if the book police needed my prints.
Death satisfies December malaise:
early darkness, a devilish wind.
Beneath my lavender flannel shroud
I drink black tea, continue to shiver.

Outside my window, a clueless sky;
even the moon looks guilty.
Tonight, I take a small break
from fiction, make a list of my own past crimes—
times I blamed myself for following the wrong path

when all along I knew my way.
What if I kill off that old self,
haul her into the frozen garden and put her down?
The weapon remains a mystery. Don't
ask me how I'll do it.

Miracle

I toss a jar of Miracle Whip into my shopping cart.
A miracle it doesn't break open. I know
how it feels to break open.

A soldier, Van Johnson, dies overseas
in the '56 film, *Miracle in the Rain*, leaving
Jane Wyman bereft. Later, he reappears—
impossibly—in front of St. Patrick's Cathedral,
embracing Jane and pledging his forever love.
Then, he's gone again.
Are miracles mostly short-lived?

Jesus miracles multiplied in catechism class.
Especially the feeding of the five thousand
with only 5 loaves, 2 fish. Or 2 loaves, 5 fish?
Miracles reverberate with numbers,
like the news.

A miracle my Grandpa Joe survived
the railroad accident that took his leg at 49.
He spun train stories, showed us where he kept
Juicy Fruit gum in a secret space in his wooden foot.
Some miracles yield a festival of delights.

Late summer. The leaves of my schefflera
houseplant are turning yellow and red
in anticipation of autumn.

I pay attention to such miracles. I'm overdue
for a signal to tear open the sun—
a gold piñata spilling gifts of light.

Pink Wig and Other Wanderings

So much news to digest. All the bad guys
coming together to hassle the world.
Sometimes I need to take a breath—
notice my dour neighbor breaking out
in a pink wig, with matching
poop bags for her Pekinese.

At Common Ground Bakery & Cafe,
Kenny Rooster is passing out flyers
for a Hen House Burlesque Show.
I don't want to limit myself
to Thursday Zumba at my local gym
while chickens in sequins flaunt their feathers.

What if Caravaggio, Raphael, da Vinci—
featured in this classy journal I'm perusing—
show up at The Charmery on 36th Street,
and overdose on Malty Vanilla Chip?
Or might a dribble of Lemon Sorbet
lighten up a brooding canvas?

On Mother's Day at church, my minister
invites the children to compose
a recipe for a Mom poem. Nouns first.
Empathy, says an older boy. Everyone nods.
What flavor is that? Pastor Steven asks.
The smallest girl whispers *Marshmallow*.

Marshmallow Empathy—the comfort I carry
into the bile of the day.

My Life According to Cocktails

Pink Squirrel: ¾ oz crème de noyaux
¾ oz white cream de cacao
1 ½ oz heavy cream
Garnish: freshly grated nutmeg
Frothy, lingerie essence, elixir of innocence.
Late teens. Still living at home.

Black Russian: 2 oz vodka
1 oz Kahlua
Dark, mysterious adventure, eau de witchcraft.
Early 20s. Immersed in the foreign playground of college.

Vodka Gimlet: 2 oz vodka
¾ oz lime juice, freshly squeezed
½ oz simple syrup
Garnish: lime wheel
Tart, tongue-startler, a glimmer of green glamour on the rim.
30s. Stronger potion for electric possibilities, setbacks, jolts.

The Chardonnay Era: Chilled bottle
Winged corkscrew
Glass/tumbler/paper cup
Crisp, aligns with career, clarity, creative awakenings.
Mid-life. Wine suits a wardrobe of happy hours.
(An occasional Margarita for spice, the salt an epiphany.)

Manhattan: 2 oz bourbon or blended
1 oz sweet vermouth
2 dashes bitters
Garnish: cherry or orange peel

Bittersweet, taste of skyscraper, skypower, a succulent buzz on the lips. Now and forever. A liquid flag waving—torn yet triumphant.

Now Eat Your Fucking Cannoli

The mobster's wife, Gina Baxter, spews out
those words with spittle and a sneer.
She shoves the plate across the table;
it strikes her man with the force of brass knuckles.
She's fed up all right. He's been slow
to enact revenge on the kid who killed
their son in a hit-and-run. Louder this time:

Eat your fucking cannoli,
the only line I recall from the whole
ten-part Netflix series.
I'm a sucker for cannoli. And the expletive helps.
A *fucking* anything seems more potent—visceral.

Dear Gina, fearless role model, volcano—
my parents and the nuns steered me
toward gentle outbursts. Like you,
I felt deeper rumblings. Losses, departures,
something broken, something blue—
needed stronger exclamations.

Rilke said, *You must change your life.*
Gina Baxter snarled, *Now eat your fucking cannoli.*
It's not the words alone.
It's the cadence, the tone, the sheer
beauty of insistence. The shout-out
from the mountain when the clouds part.

Enough mediocrity. Forget decorum,
the lady-like language of my youth:
Darn it. Dang. So help me. Oh gosh.
Now, when life boils over, I give myself
permission to curse, rant,
release a series of scorching syllables.
After I eat this cannoli,
watch out. I'll be fucking unstoppable.

My Movie Monsters

I grew up with cinematic horror. My first:
The Phantom of the Opera. The instant
that young singer ripped off Lon Chaney's mask,
all five of us—my parents, siblings, me—
leaned in. When the lights came on
we looked glued together, a human sculpture.

Along came *The Creature from the Black Lagoon,*
a prehistoric amphibian. Movie posters
flaunted the monster's taut body: electric green
with voluptuous red fish lips. It was those lips
I longed for when Dennis Shaw kissed me
on the school playground, his lips dry and chapped.

King Kong posed in glory atop an island cliff.
A gorilla meant to terrify. Still,
his lovesick eyes mesmerized. I swooned
at his enormous fist cradling Fay Wray.
I wept when New York planes shot him down.
Defying any glimmer of reason,

my best friend Rita Knipper and I sent
a sympathy card addressed to Queen Kong.
My father mailed it at the post office. We never
heard back. I pictured the widow alone
in the jungle, swinging on a single vine,
her dark chocolate face slick with grief.

My creatures died before the final credits rolled.
Did I choose poetry then,
in the basement of my childhood? You know
the moment you see something beautiful
and defend it, despite everyone else looking away.

Letter to My Younger Self

Dear Shirley,

Galileo gave you ideas, discovered rings
around Saturn. You brought them down to earth,
wore a constellation of trinkets on your fingers.
When it came to jewelry, you did everything right.

You learned to tell time on a Dali pancake watch.
Clocks alarmed; you were always late. Talking ended
your first job: stuffing envelopes at the Megiddo Mission.
I can chat and stuff, you said. You got the boot.

High school, you volunteered for the Red Cross
at an infirmary for disabled adults. You listened for hours
to garbled speech—the roots of your healing career
building bridges between lost vowels and consonants.

If only you could see your body now
wrapped in words unruly and beautiful.
Poems, your only perfume. The lingering
scent of amethyst light. Timeless.

Those rings still anchor you. You and Galileo.
At the astronomy lecture they said space is a fabric.
Somehow you already knew. You wear it
like a glittery scarf. You own the golden threads.

Love,
Yourself

Notes

"Coming of Age in Wegmans"

Wegmans is a family company/supermarket chain founded by brothers Walter and John Wegman in 1916 in my hometown of Rochester, New York.

"Roseland Park"

Roseland Park was an amusement park located on Canandaigua Lake—the 4th largest of the Finger Lakes—in upstate New York, 1925-1985.

"Sweet Dreams, Dance Man"

In memory of Jack Brock Benson: dancer, teacher, lovely man.

"Death of a Saleswoman"

Sibley, Lindsay & Curr Company, known informally as Sibley's, was a Rochester, New York-based department store chain. Its flagship store on East Main Street (1905-1990) was elegant and exquisite. The bakery was famous!

"Homeless Man Outside Walgreens"

Freddie Gray, a 25-year-old Black male, died in Baltimore, MD on April 19, 2015, from injuries suffered in police custody. Specifically, from the van ride to the police station after his questionable arrest. His death resulted in a series of violent protests in Baltimore and across the nation.

"Bobby"

Robert Francis Kennedy, RFK, Bobby—was an American politician, lawyer, and U.S. attorney general under his brother, President John F. Kennedy. Both brothers were assassinated: JFK in Dallas in 1963, RFK in Los Angeles in 1968. Bobby had just won the California primary in his own bid for the presidency, when he was shot in a kitchen hallway in the Ambassador Hotel on June 5.

"Elegy with Squeegee Boys"

Squeegee workers dart across high-traffic intersections washing windshields to earn money. Although some motorists have experienced unpleasant encounters with squeegee workers, my own experiences have always been positive. Baltimore City has begun initiatives to offer employment and workforce training to former squeegee boys.

"Cocktails with the Queen"

I have always greatly admired Queen Elizabeth II. I wrote this poem prior to the deaths of Prince Philip (April 9, 2021) and the Queen (September 8, 2022).

Queen Elizabeth's favorite handbag brand was Launer. She preferred the Royale style, and reportedly owned more than 200 Launer bags.

"It Had to Be Good to Get Where It Is"

John Stith Pemberton (July 8, 1831 – August 16, 1888) was an American pharmacist and Confederate State Army veteran who is best known as the inventor of Coca-Cola.

“My Gig as Tinsel and Beau”

Hutzler’s was a Maryland department store chain founded in 1858. The last store closed in 1990.

At Christmas, Hutzler’s featured two reindeer—Tinsel and Beau—in lieu of the more traditional Santa.

“Pat’s Dancing School”

I believe Miss Pat’s last name was “Aldrich.” I haven’t been able to find any information on her, or the dance studio. But she’s vivid in my mind! Miss Pat was definitely my idol when I was a young girl.

“Billy and Clarie, the Alligator and the Wig”

In memory of my father’s kin: William (Billy) C. Crippen and his wife of many years, Clara Mae (Clarie). Beautiful people!

“Watching Law & Order with Ted and Rezsin”

Ted Adams was my father’s first cousin. He was an eccentric and brilliant English professor who loved to read and teach poetry, although he didn’t write poems. His wife, Rezsin, was a social activist much revered in Albany, New York, where they lived. I savored my visits with them.

“Alligator at Walmart”

After a Florida news story, October 21, 2013.

Acknowledgments

Grateful acknowledgment is made to the editors of the following journals in which some of the poems first appeared, sometimes in slightly different forms:

Bay to Ocean Journal, "Goats in Wyman Park Dell," "Purple Robe, Silver Swan"

Chiron Review, "Undaunted, We Dare to Swizzle," "Manet's The Dead Toreador," "Goddess of Swizzle," "Celestial Nightmare," "It Had to Be Good to Get Where It Is," "Pink Wig and Other Wanderings," "Now Eat Your Fucking Cannoli," "Letter to My Younger Self"

Comstock Review, "A Taste of Lime," "Brush Strokes," "After Another School Shooting"

Gargoyle, "Self-Portrait in 22 Lines," "Death of a Saleswoman," "In Place of Cake," "Starry Night Diner," "Accounting," "Cubicle 4," "Endless Feast," "My Prince of Cheese," "Twist," "A Farewell to Cool Whip." "Pat's Dancing School," "You Are a Peach"

Glimpse, "Roseland Park"

Lily Poetry Review, "Breathe"

Loch Raven Review, "Poem Beginning with a Line from Richard Hugo," "The Society of Obscure Yellow Dresses," "A Treat for Joseph," "Hymn to Myself," "Ballet and Mushrooms"

Maryland Literary Review, "Homage," "At Mac's Drive-In"

Meat for Tea: The Valley Review, "Snow-Bound Mannequins," "12 Bright Oaks Drive," "My Gig as Tinsel and Beau," "Royal Dress Shop," "The Cure," "Emily Dickinson & Cher Settle In for a Heart-to-Heart," "The Center for Useless Splendor," "Billy and Clarie, the Alligator and the Wig," "Before the Last Chapter," "My Life According to Cocktails"

Naugatuck River Review, "Coming of Age in Wegmans," "After Forty-Seven Years I Remember the Cornish Hens"

New Verse News, "Dressing Room"

Paterson Literary Review, "Dear Dad," "Kitchen Couture," "Watching Law & Order with Ted and Rezsin"

Per Contra, "Sex and Utensils"

Plainsongs, "Jean and Alvina"

Poetica Review, "My Glass Slipper"

Referential, "Sweet Dreams, Dance Man"

Slant, "Elegy with Squeegee Boys"

Smartish Pace, "My Movie Monsters"

SoFloPoJo, "Cocktails with the Queen"

Tar River Poetry, "Alligator at Walmart"

The Light Ekphrastic, "Soliloquy"

The Potomac, "Urban Happy Hour"

Welter, "Gift Shop on the Arctic Circle," "Miracle"

"Keeper of the Moon," appeared in the anthology *Ice Cream Poems,* World Enough Writers, 2017

"Family Spirits" appeared in the anthology *Of Burgers and Barrooms,* Main Street Rag, 2017

"Goddess of Swizzle," reprinted in the anthology *Beer, Wine & Spirits,* World Enough Writers, 2018

"Homeless Man Outside Walgreens" appeared in the *Coffee Anthology,* World Enough Writers, 2019

"Goats in Wyman Park Dell" was nominated for a Pushcart Prize by *Bay to Ocean Journal* in 2021

"Letter to My Younger Self" was nominated for a Pushcart Prize by *Chiron*

Review in 2024

"After Forty-Seven Years I Remember the Cornish Hens" was a finalist in the annual Narrative Poetry Contest sponsored by *Naugatuck River Review* in 2024

"Pink Wig and Other Wanderings" was nominated for a Pushcart Prize by *Chiron Review* in 2025

"My Movie Monsters" received 3rd Prize, *Smartish Pace* Beullah Rose Poetry Prize, 2025

Special Thanks

With sweet gratitude to Mark Doty for the immense beauty of his mind, his kindness, and insights as a teacher.

Dollops of thanks to these friends who read, listened, and offered support/feedback:

Kathie Corcoran, Jean Flanagan, Norma Chapman, Virginia Crawford, Dan Cuddy, Dorothy Dodge, Rachel Eisler, Michael Fallon, Jenny Keith, Danka Kosk-Kosicka, Natalie Lobe, Sherry A. Morrow, Lalita Noronha, Alan Reese, Joey Reisberg, Michael Salcman, Sam Schmidt, Jim Taylor.

Chocolate sprinkles to my Poetry Zoom group: Emily Buchanan, Anne Canright, Tracey O'Rourke, Carol Tell Morse, Anastasia Vassos.

Cool Whip to the Carrot-Top Poets: Kendra Kopelke, Kathy Mangan, Sarah Merrow, Rosanne Singer, Katy Stanton, Kathleen Shemer.

Three scoops to Ron Tanner and the literary inspiration of his Good Contrivance Farm.

A crown of maraschino cherries to my three "blurbers": Sue Ellen Thompson, David Bergman, Jane Delury.

M&M's to my dedicated student editors at Apprentice House: Cecelia Durborow, Olivia DiTroia, and Emily Gott.

And marshmallow empathy to you, dear readers, for taking time to feast on my poems.

About the Poet

Shirley J. Brewer graduated from careers in bartending, palm-reading and speech therapy.

She serves as poet-in-residence at Carver Center for the Arts in Baltimore, and on the board of directors of Passager Books. She presents workshops for Passager, and for Manor Mill in Monkton.

Her award-winning poems garnish *Barrow Street, Poetry East, Slant, Gargoyle, Chiron Review*, *The Comstock Review*, and many other journals/anthologies. Shirley's books include; *A Little Breast Music* (Passager, *2008), After Words* (Apprentice House Press, 2013), *Bistro in Another Realm (*Main Street Rag, 2017), *Wild Girls* (Apprentice House Press, 2023).

Nominated four times for a Pushcart Prize, Shirley was a 2020 guest on *The Poet and The Poem* with Grace Cavalieri, former Maryland poet laureate, broadcast from the Library of Congress, where Shirley's poems are now archived and – as part of the Lunar Codex program - are currently on the moon!

Shirley received the first-ever Creativity Award from the University of Baltimore, where she earned her Master's degree in Creative Writing/Publishing Arts.

Website: shirleyjbrewer.com

Apprentice House is the country's only campus-based, student-staffed book publishing company. Directed by professors and industry professionals, it is a nonprofit activity of the Communication & Media Department at Loyola University Maryland.

Using state-of-the-art technology and an experiential learning model of education, Apprentice House publishes books in untraditional ways.This dual responsibility as publishers and educators creates an unprecedented collaborative environment among faculty and students, while teaching tomorrow's editors, designers, and marketers.

Outside of class, progress on book projects is carried forth by the AH Book Publishing Club, a co-curricular campus organization supported by Loyola University Maryland's Office of Student Activities.

Eclectic and provocative, Apprentice House titles intend to entertain as well as spark dialogue on a variety of topics. Financial contributions to sustain the press's work are welcomed.Contributions are tax deductible to the fullest extent allowed by the IRS.

To learn more about Apprentice House books or to obtain submission guidelines, please visit www.apprenticehouse.com.

Apprentice House Press
Communication & Media Department
Loyola University Maryland
4501 N. Charles Street
Baltimore, MD 21210
Ph: 410-617-5265
info@apprenticehouse.com•www.apprenticehouse.com

www.ingramcontent.com/pod-product-compliance
Lightning Source LLC
LaVergne TN
LVHW010625100826
845148LV00014B/3115

9781627206242